Lightning in the Mind

Aaron Christensen

USA • Canada • UK • Ireland

Note for Librarians: A cataloguing record for this book is available from Library and Archives Canada at www.collectionscanada.ca/amicus/index-e.html
ISBN 1-4120-6769-3

Printed on paper with minimum 30% recycled fibre. Trafford's print shop runs on "green energy" from solar, wind and other environmentally-friendly power sources.

Offices in Canada, USA, Ireland and UK
This book was published *on-demand* in cooperation with Trafford Publishing. On-demand publishing is a unique process and service of making a book available for retail sale to the public taking advantage of on-demand manufacturing and Internet marketing. On-demand publishing includes promotions, retail sales, manufacturing, order fulfilment, accounting and collecting royalties on behalf of the author.

Book sales for North America and international:
Trafford Publishing, 6E–2333 Government St.,
Victoria, BC V8T 4P4 CANADA
phone 250 383 6864 (toll-free 1 888 232 4444)
fax 250 383 6804; email to orders@trafford.com
Book sales in Europe:
Trafford Publishing (UK) Limited, 9 Park End Street, 2nd Floor
Oxford, UK OX1 1HH UNITED KINGDOM
phone 44 (0)1865 722 113 (local rate 0845 230 9601)
facsimile 44 (0)1865 722 868; info.uk@trafford.com
Order online at:
trafford.com/05-1680

10 9 8 7 6 5 4 3 2 1

Ackknowledgements

Thanks to photographer, Linda Menke, for the cover picture. This picture has been altered and was taken during April of 1987 atop of "the Rock." This "Rock," also happens to be the rock where my brother Andy's ashes were spread, by my immediate family and myself, into the Pacific ocean.

Thank you Andy for all of your inspiration, love and courage. Not a day goes by without thoughts and memories of you. You don't know how incredibly difficult and sad life has been without you here. You are missed immensely and will never be forgotten. I love you Andy.

Thank you Rico for your rich stories, outlook on life and for always telling me to hang in there and keep with the Aloha Spirit. Cheka Looka!

Contents

Offbeat

Lyrical

Nature

A Super Friend

Honor

A Teardrop

A teardrop rolls down my cheek,
as I take a long, deep breath.

Please, take with you, my heart
and only love . . . . unto one another.
Please, take with you, my spirit
and blessedly touch many spirits.

Take with you, my eyes
to only see the love and the beauty.
Take with you, my passion
and achieve your highest dreams.

And take with you, my courage
and dare to be, not so fearful.
And take with you, my hope
so you do not ever despair.

A teardrop rolls down my cheek,
as I give you all, all that I may have.

A teardrop rolls down my cheek,
as I kiss you all, a final kiss goodbye.

In Honor of Andy Christensen.

Time Drifts By

Doesn't seem real at times,
he was just right here.
I know he's gone,
it's just hard to believe.

Ashes from my hands,
from atop a mighty rock,
falling into the waves
and crashing into space.

This is where my
brother rests . . . .
This is where my
friend rests . . . .

Time drifts by . . . .
Time drfits by . . . .

He may not be here?
Oh, I'm not so sure,
for I've felt his prescence . . . .
and I've seen him . . . . for sure.

Yes, he's here, I'm sure.

This is where my
brother rests . . . .

This is where my
friend rests . . . .

Time drifts by . . . .
Time drifts by . . . .

In honor of Andy Christensen.

Why did you die, my friend? Why?
Why is this happening?

Why did you take your own life, my friend?
Why?

Why do I cry?

Why were you chosen to die, my friend? Why?
Why do I love you my friend?

Why do I hurt?

Why am I here?

Why did you die my brother? Why?
Why did you leave?

Why do I cry?

Why do you hurt, my brother?
Why are you sick, my brother?
Why aren't you outside, playing with your
friends, my brother?

Why did you die, Andy? Why?
Why aren't you alive?

Why did I hit you, my brother?
Why do I cry?

Why do I love you my brother?

Why?

Fourteen

April 13, 1984, out with my friends,
Saturday night on my birthday.
Eight months ago, my closest brother
died of cancer, at age fourteen.

We mixed gin and orange juice
in a glass jar.
Taking turns,
we all drank the concoction.
We were all giddy and laughing
as we finished the intoxicating drink.

We then uncorked a bottle of champagne
. . . . it was gone within a few minutes.

We walked to a park,
drunk with pleasure
and rode around on the
merry go-round.

My girlfriend and I
broke away
and fell into some bushes.
We kissed for a while.

We eventually started
walking back to the house . . . .
I could barely walk . . . .
let alone stand.

It was the first time
I'd been drunk . . . .
and it was the first time
I kissed a girl . . . .

I was fourteen . . . .

Our Sun Shines

Luminous clouds
sailing high and smooth,
a reflection of their beauty
in a quiet pond.

As the heavens look down
upon many sad spirits,
love laiden tears
stream down
our faces,
pelting the earth.

A loving friend
has taken her peace now . . . .

And forever
shall we keep
her love
deep inside us.

The rain does not come
on this day . . . .

No, the rain
does not come
today.

For our spirits are strong,
with loving warmth,
and they will not fade
like an everlasting summer.

High in the heavens,
a sun shines . . . .
and our sun shines.

Underneath the clouds,
a sun shines . . . .
as our sun shines.

In memory of Debbie.

Love

Dance in the Sky

Dance with your soul
in the warm summer night,
fly to a peaceful heaven
as swiftly as you can.

My eyes catch a glimpse
of your fleeting beauty,
and for just a moment,
all my fears are unmasked.

Dance in the sky,
fly with your love . . . .
Dance in the sky,
and fly with our love.

A quiet butterfly, so sacred,
moves with gentle ease . . . .
you float nearby,
clasping my heart with your love.

We slowly drift upwards,
dancing together in rhythm,
with nothing to stop us,
and our love in the sky.

Dance in the sky,
fly with your love . . . .
Dance in the sky,
and fly with our love.

Dizzy Sense

Walking in a manner
coming closer to heaven,
eluding my gypsy soul
with your starlight trance.

Your flame grows strong
as you're almost gone,
my deep aching desire
is to feel your burning fire.

I've got a dizzy sense . . . .
Oh . . . . Oh . . . .
I've got a dizzy sense of you . . . .

Rising to my limits
as I breathe in your beauty,
inhaling your power
like a fragrant flower.

The sun rolls away
as you slip into the clouds.
Well, I'm gone with you now . . . .

inside those clouds . . . .
till the end of time . . . .
inside those clouds . . . .
till the end of time . . . .

Lavender Pisces

The scent of lavender,
a loving Pisces,
luscious lips
dripped in passion.

Red roses
dropped in your path,
my heart pulsates
faster and faster.

The arduous strife
of this strong
battling ram
must come to an end, now . . . .

. . . . continue your healing
. . . . continue this heaven

You are a bright star
with hot sizzling flames,
melting this frozen statue
and bringing forth
vigorous, sexual life.

Torrid emotions run rampid
as sweet lavender mist,
kisses this cursed
and demonic soul.

. . . . continue your healing
. . . . continue this heaven

The bleeding sacrifice
of your touch . . . .

creates screams and cries
heard from within . . . .

. . . . and the silent signs of fate

beckon for another
escape, with . . . .

the Lavender Pisces.

Tsunami of Love

A torcherous amount
of anticipation
building over
the years.

Like a ripple
of love
growing
with every thought
of you.

My heart yearns
deeply
for your
presence.

Stranded at sea
for so long,
as my ripple
of love grows and grows
with rich, passion
and deep desires.

Fighting everyday
to stay strong,
as immense
feelings
soon turn

this ripple
of love
into a tsunami.

And as your
feelings are alike,
another ripple of love
is turned into a
tsunami of passion.

And our two Tsunamis meet,
crashing wildly
into each other,
creating
an endless . . . .
sea
of
love.

Transcending Dream

Upwards and inwards
you gaze into my soul,
looking to my spirit
with your beautiful eyes.

A tender young heart
awaiting a romance,
a face so sweet
and carved of beauty.

This is our transcending dream,
we are laughing
and we are loving.

Under the sky and stars
our love becomes eternal,
as a single kiss to the lips
awakens our tranquil love.

As sun shines on our souls
in the cool morning air,
a new life begins to breathe
into this transcending dream.

This is our transcending dream,
we are kissing
and we are hugging.

Speak Your Love

Deepen your love,
so you may see
a beautiful spirit,
awaken with life.

Speak softly
with your love,
and smile with
your innocent bliss.

Walk slowly, gently . . . .
and I will do my best
to follow . . . .
with as nice a grace.

Sleep quietly tonight
and dream sweetly,
in this beautiful haven
of our sacred love.

Speak your love
with a smile . . . .
Speak your love . . . .
and stay awhile.

The First Time

The first time
I saw you,
there was immediate
physical attraction.

Your beautiful, dark coffee eyes
and silky, feathered, ebony hair . . . .

. . . . toned, muscular calves
and sultry hips. . . .

. . . . high cheek bones
and silky, moist lips . . . .

. . . . a tight abdomen,
and prominent firm,
round breasts.

Your movements
mimmicked an
exotic elegance
and perfect grace.

Your energy, so
spiritually stimulating
and erroticly intense.

We catch each
others eyes
and there's
nervousness in our
voices as we
begin to speak.

We talk
for an hour
asking questions
about each other . . . .

. . . . and so soon the
time dwindles down,
for us to say
our goodbyes.

We say our goodbyes
to each other. . . .

. . . . and I still wonder,
what it will
be like
when we
kiss . . . .

. . . . for the
first time.

Love, for Nothing

oh, Love,
where did you go?

how have I lost you?
before I even knew you?

Temptrists' eyes with
angelic flowing hair,
delicate curves, so round
and soft to the touch . . . .

is it too much Love for me?

what happened sweetheart?
did I steal your last meal?

you are absolute heaven
in my arms . . . .

something,
which I have not had
for a long, long time . . . .

come near me,
whisper in my ear
with your sweet voice,

let me hear you,
feel you,
near me . . . .

your senses Love?
what do you feel?
do you feel anything inside?

are you afraid . . . . afraid of my feelings?

please speak,
so I understand . . . .
don't push me away . . . .
for nothing.

for nothing . . . .
I wouldn't give
to be with you,
in my arms . . . . now.

. . . . my lips, my heart
are waiting for you . . . .

my heart is heavy,
sunken into despair . . . .
for nothing?

oh love . . . . oh love . . . .
my heart . . . . it beats . . . .
for nothing . . . . for nothing . . . .

. . . . A Light Shines

on two stangers,
as we meet . . . .
in a dark room . . . .
adjusting to the mood.

an awkward stance . . . .
yet, knowing it's ok .

unforgiving are my errors
. . . . as a light shines.

can you somehow?
brushing up near me . . . .
repair this crushed heart?

silence speaking so beautifully . . . .
. . . . as a light shines

feeling by looking
. . . . a light shines
looking for love

letting go now
for you . . . .

. . . . a light shines
showing all the tears

. . . . a light shines
showing all fears

yet, there are none . . . .

only . . . . a light,

. . . . a light that shines,
on two strangers.

waiting for . . . .

I've been waiting . . . .
and waiting for . . . . you.

I've seen all the signs,
there is no mistake . . . .

. . . . you are finally with me
and we are fine.

. . . . the signs

. . . . you are gone now,
though I'm the one that left.

I want you back now
and there is no mistake . . . .

for you aren't with me
and I'm not fine . . . .

Yet, I'll keep waiting . . . .
and waiting . . . .

. . . . because I see
all of the signs.

set me free . . . .

set me free. . . .

tonight,
there is no
better time . . . .

harvest moon
in the window,
dark shadows rustling
on the wall . . . .

silk sheets . . . .
candles . . . .
pulses . . . .

set me free . . . .

night into morning
and morning into night . . . .

set me free . . . .

you smile, cry and laugh . . . .
be free with me . . . .

set me free . . . .

make me believe . . . .
there's a heaven
for me . . . . be free . . . .

set me free . . . .

when you smile

I am in so much disbelief.
My head shakes
as I envision
your beautiful smile.

how can you be so beautiful?

would you still
be so beautiful,
had you a scar
on your face?

if you couldn't hear, see or talk?

would I still see you as the same person?

soft, curly black hair,
gentle, soothing voice,
radiant, chestnut eyes.

I see your heart when you smile . . . .
I see an angel when you smile . . . .

that is what is special to me . . . .
your loving, caring heart.

what is in your heart?
I would like to find out.

who is this angel
with the beautiful smile?

will you please let me into your world?

Two Souls Together

Autumn breeze
blowing through our hair,
red and gold leaves
floating in the air.

Autumn breeze
blowing through the trees,
whispering there's love
for you and me.

The stars up above
glisten in the night,
as we gaze and dream
at the heavenly sight.

Our lips soon embrace
and our passion unites,
our two souls together
as one love for the night.

Moonlight shines down
upon our rapturous souls,
as thunderous waves
crash down upon the shore.

Loving each other
in the cool evening mist,
our two souls together
as one infinte kiss.

A Chance Taken

A quiet, lonely
and early morning
signals a wonderous destiny,
as long as, there's a chance . . . .

a chance taken . . . .

She looks your way
with a beautiful gaze
and alluring pose,
vying to get your
attention,
for just a
split second . . . .

a chance taken . . . .
is not forsaken . . . .
it's a chance taken . . . .

You catch her glance,
with provocative curiosity,
she is curious . . . .
as you are furious . . . .
with virility and stamina.

You walk up to her
and whisper a lover's
great secret in her ear.

She brushes up
against you, and
both bodies become
excited , hot and electric.

"I am with you now,"
she whispers . . . .
"as you are with me."

A Chance Taken

-revisited

A quiet early morning,
another lonely day,
that soon shall pass,
unless, there's a chance . . . .

. . . . taken,
and not forsaken.
Yes, a chance taken.

She looks your way
with her beautiful eyes,
alluring to the look.
You get a quick glance
of her sultry posture,
leaning up against a counter.

It's the woman you love.
As you slowly move to her,
the chemistry ignites
and you capture
her essence and soul, with . . . .

A chance taken . . . .

. . . . torrid love
rushes around the room
like a tempest . . . .

. . . . as we knock down
everyting
in our path,
leaving nothing,
except . . . .

. . . . a chance taken.

Pain

The Night

Down and out,
no place to go,
not much money,
not a friend to call.

Battling these demons
inside my head,
fighting for another day and
praying for this hell to end.

The sun diminishes
and the cold, ominous darkness
suddenly strikes,
into my horrible
world of pain.

. . . . my senses
panic and tremble . . . .

And still, the night goes on . . . .

. . . . litter, scattered around
a desolate lamp post . . . .

. . . . with, no mercy, for this murder.

Leave . . . .

my father,
I still love you,
as I know life as no different.

Leave, my brother,
you have fought hard
and long enough . . . .
and have showed us all
the true meaning of courage.

Leave, my childhood,
for you are now,
just a distant and joyful memory.

Leave, my brother,
for your world has arrived,
and it needs to be explored.

Leave again, my father,
and may your absence,
make this man grow stronger yet.

Leave, my mother,
for your grief
seems too great to overcome,
for any mortal.
No, you are stronger than most.

Leave, my brother,
"Oh . . . . thank GOD!
You're still here!"

Leave, my senses,
for I am lost now,
and do not know where you are.

Leave, my sweetheart,
for I have been taken
by another.

Leave, my friend,
your sweetheart is
waiting for your kiss.

Leave, my hell
for I have seen, way
too much of you . . . .

and, it's now time
to see a bit . . . .
of Heaven!

The Love I Lost

You came into my life
without a moments notice,
and soon became
the sparkle in my eyes.

You made my life complete
as happy as I'd been.
I finally saw the light
I thought would never shine.

Ah love . . . .
Love . . . .

Now the passion in my heart
beats for another loving soul,
as the deep pain and sadness
is hidden all too well.

My thoughts are with you
wherever you may be,
and though I choose to love,
it is still not the answer.

Oh, my love . . . . is lost
My love . . . . is lost
Gone now, is the
love I lost . . . .

Farewell To Your Love

To bid farewell
to the one you love
may not come
as easy as you'd like.

For you've lived
to cherish your love,
as though no other
could change that sentiment.

Yet, your heart
comes unto another,
and suddenly,
your world
is turned upside down.

With bitter sorrow
and painful regret,
the courage finally comes
to bid farewell
to your love.

Though the chance
doesn't come,
for your love is gone . . . .
and the past,
quickly becomes a reminder
of a farewell not bid.

Time of Dying

There shall be no tears
in my time of dying,
for there shall be
no time to shed them.

All this pain and sorrow
shall be gone, as well as
all the fighting
to be strong and courageous.

Long at last, I will fly
free with wings,
singing happily in peace,
as I ought and please.

The heavy pounding
in this wounded
and aching heart,
along with all
the bitter angst,
finally, shall be gone, forever.

And so, when this spirit
shall arise,
in my time of dying,
let another spirit
soon arrive . . . .
with only more . . . .
love . . . . to give.

Sad Song

Sitting on the bridge
with the sun on our backs,
letting the time pass
while feeling out our lives . . . .

Smoking a cigarette
with not too many worries,
wondering how we might
make a chance, turn out right . . . .

Fifteen years old
listening to music,
no plans for the future,
just plans for the night . . . .

Seeking a thrill . . . .
jumping from a bridge . . . .
it ends with a splash . . . .

Getting high and drunk
with no morals at hand,
as dreams come and go . . . .
a heart still mourns . . . .

From deep down inside
you fight the screams . . . .
for all you want is now . . . .
not some dead end road . . . .

Sad Song

-revisited

Sitting on a bridge
the sun on our backs,
letting the time pass
while feeling out our lives.
Smoking a cigarette,
throwing down a cold one,
and wondering how our dreams
just might turn out . . . .

Listening to music
with all of your friends,
jumping from a bridge
three stories high, just for a thrill.
Keeping happy now
with no plans for a future,
just not wanting
a dead end road . . . .

Now you're older
yet still hear the screams,
though now, the screams
come deep from within . . . .
not heard by anyone
except yourself . . . .
and this, is where the
fighting begins . . . .

Offbeat

Slipping Away

It's just a bit further now,
I can sense it,
yet . . . . it's nowhere in sight.

A dream so real . . . .
A dream so close . . . .

Yet, I feel, it's slipping away.

I hold on so tight
to every bit of hope.

A glimmer in my heart
creating a new spark . . . .

. . . . wanting to forge on
. . . . for a bit more

The day is hot,
as I rest awhile
in the cool shade . . . .
obtaining a glimpse
of the dream
quietly being achieved.

Falling into a deep slumber . . . .
my memory searches
for a new path,

a new picture,
to reach for . . . .
to grasp hold of . . . .
for a guide.

Yet, nothing is found.

Just old and beaten
traveled paths,
leading to places
visited by no one.

A man is stirred
from his deep slumber . . . .
so much
wanting to find his way,
find his dream . . . .
that is . . . .
his dream . . . .
that is . . . .
slipping away.

Keep on Truckin'

God, I've been here
a long time!
Way too long!

It's mile marker 20
again, and
I'm hittin' the wall!

Keep on truckin'!

It's a marathon
I'm runnin',
and the finish line
is near . . . .

Keep going strong!
Keep on truckin'!

One heartbeat at a time,
one step at a time.
I'll finish . . . .
Oh yes, I'll get there!

Keep on truckin'!

Stay focused,
Yah, that's right!
Tough it out!
Just keep on moving

to get past
the pain!

Keep on truckin'!

"You can do it,
yes you can!
You can do it,
I know you can!"

Oh, the pain . . . .
Oh, the agony . . . .

endorphins release . . . .
endorphins release . . . .

Keep on truckin' . . . .
Keep on truckin' . . . .

Find a Way

You might find a way . . . .
find your own way.

You might find the truth . . . .
find your true self.

You may find heaven . . . .
find your soulmates.

You may find peace . . . .
find your silence.

You might find happiness . . . .
find your laugh.

You might find a friend . . . .
find a few.

You may find sometimes . . . .
it's harder than you think.

Yes, find a way,
and know it's true . . . .

Find a way,
and make sure it's you.

Reflections

Play while you're still young.

Fall in love during Autumn.

Wrestle in a pile of fallen leaves.

Splash in the gutters on rainy days.

Dream away with your passionate heart.

Climb a mountain and enjoy the view.

Swim in the surf and laugh a lot.

Lay in the sun on a hot summer day.

Kiss a friend and say, "I love you."

Walk on the beach and feel the cool breeze.

Sit in silence and be at peace.

Listen to the birds' harmonious songs.

Hug a tree with awe and wonder.

Find a great escape and read a book.

Spirituality

striving and reaching
for a
last chance
leaning
on a star
to stir up
more energy
a pure spirit
at last
nothing left
untethered
Mozart playing
in the wind
with time
in the mind
a constant drizzling
between frames
rapid ascension
sets the heart
free
melting
all of the angst
the crescendoes
and dissapation
of tones
weathers
the euphoric
spirit . . . .
. . . . which enters
a final
transformation
so majestic
only a world
far, far away
could be
imagined . . . .

Spirituality -revisited

striving and reaching
for a last chance
leaning on a star
to gain new energy
a pure spirit at last
and so untethered

playing in the wind
and on time
with Mozart
the drizzling of tones
continues as a constant
while a heart is set free
with the descending and ascending
of peaceful notes

a final transformation
of a spirit, believing of itself
clinging to a burning belief . . . .
. . . . a voice is heard
and must be answered to
before . . . . the others call.

Maybe this infinite sky
will stay young and beautiful?

Maybe this roaming sea
will remain powerful and wise?

Maybe this bitter life
will continue with grief and pain?

Maybe these wild dreams
will come true as the seasons change.

Maybe this great escape
will turn into peace of mind?

Maybe you, my love
will keep smiling and waiting?

Maybe . . . . maybe . . . .

Angel in Disguise

Watching with your
falcon eyes,
you don't miss
a beat . . . .

your patience
is beyond your years . . . .

no arms, no fears . . . .

You wonder how
the battles are conquered . . . .

Covering
the pains
and deep scars
with constant
choices
of healing love . . . .

An angel in disguise,
not ready
for the light
of a new day . . . .
or a new beginning . . . .

Perservering with
your mission,
as someone

watches in amazement
you come so near . . . .

I want to touch you,
yet, you're miles
and miles away,
or at least a few
years . . . .

An angel in disguise, with
no wings to fly . . . .

An angel in disguise and
not going to cry . . . .

How do you cry?

The time has come
for the disguise
to be gone . . . .

. . . . and one should
only wonder,
what has now
just begun . . . .

Six Tracks

red lights flashing
six tracks in front

a bright moon overhead
six tracks below

silver clouds pass on by
six tracks

loud bells with
constant ringing
back and forth

she lays in bed
dreaming
of a night
with this man
who just let
her out
of this world

six tracks in front
six tracks below
six tracks

Lyrical

Looking for My Love

Looking to the east
for my love, oh yah!
Looking to the west
for my dear, oh yah!

Went to the east
for my love, uh huh!
Went to the west
for my dear, uh huh!

She wasn't across the river
where I thought she'd be!
She wasn't past the mountains
near the honeybees!

Looking for my love
Oh, yes indeed!
Looking for my dear
Oh, yes indeed!

Well, I found my love
Oh yes, I did indeed!
My dear's right here with me,
where she said she'd be!

Time to get (a little) Funny . . . .

Just sittin' here thinkin',
how life can be kind of rough.
So, when the going gets tough,
it's time to get a little . . . .

silly . . . .
smiley . . . .
sassy . . . .
Funny . . . .

Oh, life can also be short,
yah, sometimes very damn short.
So, if you think you've had it,
it's time to get a little . . .

saucy . . . .
jazzy . . . .
funky . . . .
Funny . . . .

If you're not a lovin',
If you're not a playin',
and, if you're not a laughin',
then, it's time to get a little . . . .

silly . . . . saucy . . . .
jazzy . . . .jazzy . . . .
funky . . . .sassy . . . .
Funny . . . . Funny . . . .

One for Fun

Sweet lyrics and luscious melodies
coming from endless creativity,
invitations to delve and go deep,
into our music you will seep.

We keep a nice even beat
as you move your fancy feet,
to our new and fantastic sounds
of hip-hop stylin' on the streets.

Boys and girls the time is now
to get moving with our beat,
cause you're feelin' really groovy
and you just won't sit still.

Keep a movin' and a shakin'
cause were not stoppin' yet,
till you get crazy and wild
and make it a night you won't forget.

Jazz, soul, & rock-n-roll,
rap, funk, rhythm & blues,
all mixed as one . . . . one for fun . . .

New Love

Take the long, sharp sliver
out of my bleeding heart.
You say you love me
yet, I continue to bleed.

You take my heart
without a second thought,
not seeming to care
and thinking that's all right.

Well, I've got a new love
a dream girl so real . . . .
She's a great lovin' gal,
right here by my side.

She talks in a way
in which I understand,
a way, in which you
won't ever understand.

She brings out a part of me
that's non-existant with you,
that's where the pain is
and so shall remain.

Yes, I've got a new love
a dream girl so real . . . .
She's a great lovin' gal,
forever by my side.

I Know a Girl

I know a girl
who I want to say "Hi" to!
She's got long, black hair
with cinnamon eyes!

When she looks at me
with her beautiful smile,
I smile back at her
and love's on my mind!

Her name is Annika!
She has a sweet voice.
She loves to smile.
Her name is Annika!

We're going to the hills
the countryside so far,
we're going to make a fire
to keep us nice and warm!

We're going to tell some stories
and we're going to sing & laugh!
Oh . . . . we're starting to kiss!

Oh, I know a girl,
Her name is Annika!
Yah, I know a girl,
Yes, her name is Annika!

Little Sweet Bee

I'll bet you never knew!
Oh, I'll bet you never knew!
Yes, I'll bet you never knew,
about the Love I've had for you!

I'm giving you lovin'!
Oh, I'm giving you my lovin'!
Yes, you're my Little Sweet Bee!
And, I'm giving you my lovin'!

I love you in the morning!
Oh, I love you in the morning!
Yes, I've got a whole lot of loving,
for my Sweet Bee in the morning!

I'm walking on the clouds!
Oh, I'm walking on the clouds!
I'm so in love with you,
my Little Sweet Bee,
that I'm walking on the clouds!

I love my Sweet Bee!
Oh, yes I do!
Oh, my Honey's sweet!
Ooh ooh ooh!

Nature

Vietnamese Moon

High above the clouds
looming skyward,
through bamboo branches,
a crescent moon shines
it's light down upon us.
Like the song Saigon,
flowing slow and smooth,
the moon moves, as
a dancers' silent grace . . . .

Riding along a dirt road . . . .
with my arms clasped
around your waist.
Dark hair, blowing past my face,
the wind whistling . . . . in our ears.

. . . . we settle on a sandy bank
of the song Saigon,
and look up at the vivid,
crescent shape in the dark sky.

We look into each others eyes,
as our exotic lips
press firmly upon each others . . . .

for a moment . . . .
time stops . . . .
as a Vietnamese Moon
shines upon us.

Whisper in the Wind

A willow sways softly
to and fro in a gentle breeze.

A lover whispers in the wind.

Maple leaves turned
a golden hue
descend,
until caressing
the cool heavenly earth.

A soft deep sigh is heard from afar.

Oaks and pines
moan throughout the night,
their branches
twisting and turning . . . .

Dark clouds loom above,
expelling a fury
of deafening thunder . . . .

A lover whispers in the wind.
A soft, deep sigh is heard from afar.

A fresh new rain,
pelts the outstretched
leaves and branches.

Lightning bolts crackle
in the sullen night . . . .

And a lover whispers in the wind.

Autumnal Equinox

The leaves of summer
have fallen again,
as the Autumnal equinox
draws near.

The past green colors
of Spring, now orchestrate
an alluring display
of brilliant oranges,
cinnamon and maroon.

The warm sun
tanning the fall leaves,
settles just below
two snow-capped peaks.

A blusterous gust of wind
blows across a prairie,
rustling the fallen leaves
into wild and twirling frenzies.

The beautiful colors
move across the prairie,
like passionate lovers
embraced in a dance.

The leaves now
scatter peacefully
on to a rivers surface . . . .
. . . . finally taking
a resting place
along it's quiet
and sandy banks.

Snow Falling

Soon, the snow begins to fall,
drifting ever so lightly . . . .
from the cold and dark heavens,
into the lonely valley.

Birds once singing in the trees
are now gone . . . .
the quiet, rolling hills
stretched side by side,
are all barren
and can be seen
for miles and miles.

Snowflakes gently settle
on to an old window sill . . . .
a caretaker, gone sometime now,
has left a window open.

Evening settles in, as
the daylight starts to fade . . . .
an air of innocence meanders
through the silent cottage . . . .
and nothing stirs,
as time becomes a memory . . . .
and the memory quickly disappears
to the sound, of a distant,
echoing train whistle.

Jupiter's on the Horizon

Jupiter's on the horizon,
three moons encircling the star
. . . . with a saphire glow . . . .
speckled dust dances,
illuminating the distant landscape
of the million mile star, Styanmar.

Mountains and craters
enshrouded . . . .
hills and valleys
covered . . . .
by pockets of dense
and dark moving fog.

While darkness slowly arrives
a westerly squall picks up,
littering crusted moon rocks
into lakes of silver liquid.

Jupiter disappears
into a swirling
black mass . . . .
as stars and nothingness
entrance a wandering soldier.

. . . . time passes away
and a dreamy Jupiter
appears again, on the horizon.

Sunset

Beside the river,
beside the ocean,
beside the jagged rocks,
and behind pink and orange clouds
the sun glides down . . . .

Belonging like the
sun and the clouds,
our two yearning hearts
are no longer alone.

A beautiful evening
awaits for our love
to intwine and for
our destiny to unravel . . . .

We look to the horizon
as we hold each other tight,
as the bright star
says goodbye to the day.

Dark and looming
before us . . . .
James Island,
rests calmly
among the ocean's
crashing waves . . . .

Seagulls soaring
majestically
through the air,
coast in the wind,
and come to perch on
the top of some island crags.

The ocean spray
lightly mists the driftwood,
as the sun dips
below the sea . . . .
beckoning for us to
continue our
eve of loving . . . .

The sky is full of shooting stars.

Our spirits ascend
attaining peaceful bliss,
as we are surrounded
by this beautiful sunset.

. . . . Upon the Rialto

Our hearts pound
with passion,
as we embrace and kiss
. . . . upon the Rialto.

The crescent moon
shines down,
as we lay, side by side
. . . . upon the Rialto.

Thunderous waves
echo all night,
as we make love
. . . . upon the Rialto.

A beautiful rapture
comes upon us,
feeling the cool wind
blowing across the Rialto.

We collide harmoniously,
listening to the melodic sounds
. . . . upon the Rialto.

We fall asleep
in each others arms,
as we dream again
. . . . upon the Rialto.

A Super Friend

If You Only Knew . . . .

If you only knew . . . .
how long I've been in love with you.
You could wake up
and take a step out
of your fantasy world.

If you only knew . . . .
how I've longed, to feel
your passionate heart at night.
You could stop being afraid
and start to feel, the
love blossom inside.

If you only knew . . . .
how I'd like to change
some of my poor
and wretched choices.
You might just forgive me,
laugh, smile and let me know
. . . . it's ok.

If you only knew . . . .
what I've felt for so long,
though have not ever expressed.
You might listen . . . .
. . . . and then say it yourself.

I love you.

Madison Street

We were alone alas
that quiet night
in June.
A warm evening
so young,
with gentle touches
and smiles.

A sea breeze
stimulating
our love,
with sudden
cool gusts.

My thoughts
went elsewhere,
and so quickly
did I lose . . . .
a pleasurable and
loving escape . . . .
turned into
pain and disbelief.

Not a day nor night
goes by,
without thoughts
of that evening.

Your sweet kiss
on my cheek,
reminds me
of a nice dream.

Please forgive
my poor choices
made as I was
near blind . . . .
and let me come
to you now,
as it were that
night again, on . . . .

. . . . Madison street.

Heartbeats

Follow your true hearts desires!
Dance to your rhythm of love!
Come with me, let's tango!
Feel my heartbeat against yours!

You are the passion
in my heart!
You are the sweet taste
in my mouth!
A melody
hummed so lusciously!
A joyful tear
rolling down my cheek!

You epitomize my true love!
A treasure to hold deep in my heart!
A soulmate with exquiste taste!
The beauty of all my dreams!

Our heartbeats dance
with the sunshine,
as our hands our clasped tight.

You are so beautiful . . . .
I love you.

A Wild, Purple Orchid

The fragrance of a
wild spring flower
attracts a young, sweet bee
foraging for pollen.

The sun shines down
on the blossoms
fresh with dew,
bringing a mild warmth
to the bee's
early dawn flight.

The flowers offer her
a plentiful supply of pollen,
as she scours about
with a pleasant buzzing.

She finds her way inside
a wild, purple orchid,
and is soon intoxicated
with the magic of purple.

Their lips meet,
as he kisses the sweet bee,
and with that kiss
she sighs and swoons.

And with the touch
of the wild orchid's
loving stamen,
she finds heaven's delights
in a grove of
wild orchids.

Taking the delightful pollen
from the wild orchid,
the sweet bee
is refreshed again
with love, now . . . .
and forever.

Secret Obsession

The eyes in my mind
create a vision of you
. . . . radiant silver mist
swirls around . . . .

Seeing your smile
brings a steady beat
to my heart.

We gradually begin
to walk toward each other.

All of these waning years,
months, days, weeks,
minutes and seconds,
coming together now
as a fiery affair
of anticipation.

A life beckons us
filled with magic
and enlightenment . . . .
a force, pulling
us closer together,
in a loving cradle.

For a few seconds,
the sun peaks out
from the clouds,
and I am warmed,
and reminded,
of my present reality . . . .

awoken from
my . . . .
Secret Obsession.

Sweethearts

Falling further away
with teardrops in my eyes,
you were so close
and yet, I didn't see you.

Your eyes always sparkled
with laughter and love,
while your spirit was filled
with passion and romance.

Let's dance one more dance,
to a slow, romantic song . . . .
let's blend our hearts
to make one beautiful love.

Let our hearts feel light,
let us rise to the heavens . . . .
let's share our love,
let's enjoy the night.

Let's sleep in peace,
let's dream sweet dreams . . . .
and awake in loving joy,
so we can fall in love
. . . . all over again.

I'm Listening . . . .

. . . . to the sound
of your voice
as you say,
"I love you."

My heart cries,
as I say
"I love you too."

I've loved you
all this time,
while we've been apart . . . .
all those years elapsed . . . .
sad, regretful, angry feelings . . . .
It doesn't matter now,
for you've brought me
my heaven.

Are my eyes not mistaken?
Capturing all of the beauty,
wonder and awe
of the universe . . . .
Simply . . . .
your heart, mind and soul.

I'm listening to your heart . . . .
listening . . . . to your love . . . .
I'm listening . . . . at last.

Why . . . .

. . . . don't we fall in love again?

Like we did
so long ago,
on a warm summer day.

The sunshine
beaming on our faces,
smiling at each other
and laughing
with energy
so full of
Love.

A Kiss

A kiss in the morning,
to start a beautiful day.

A soft kiss on the cheek,
on the corner of the street.

A romantic kiss in the park,
under silver stars in the dark.

A long kiss in the rain,
drenching our quenched souls.

A passionate kiss by the fire,
as we warm our tender hearts.

A loving kiss goodnight to you,
my one and only true love.

A heavenly kiss in a dream,
while asleep in each other's arms.

An infinite kiss of love,
is all that is left for us now.

A Beautiful Dawn

Music to my ears is the sound of your laugh.

Every night in your arms, in a quiet,
loving heaven.

Love, from now till eternity, is my gift for you.

In the dawn, rain or shine, a wonderful
romance awaits.

Sweetheart's on my mind, with a kiss on the way.

Singing about my true love, brings me
peace and harmony.

Always, there will be the beautiful thought
of you . . . .

www.ingramcontent.com/pod-product-compliance
Ingram Content Group UK Ltd.
Pitfield, Milton Keynes, MK11 3LW, UK
UKHW041928190726
13854UKWH00004B/1509

9 781412 067690